LIFE CYCLE OF AN...

Oak Tree

Revised and Updated

Angela Royston

Heinemann Library
Chicago, Illinois

www.heinemannraintree.com
Visit our website to find out more information about Heinemann-Raintree books.

To order:
☎ Phone 888-454-2279
🖥 Visit www.heinemannraintree.com to browse our catalog and order online.

Edited by Adrian Vigliano, Harriet Milles, and Diyan Leake
Designed by Kimberly R. Miracle and Tony Miracle
Original illustrations © Capstone Global Library Limited
  2001, 2009
Illustrated by Alan Fraser
Picture research by Tracy Cummins and Heather Mauldin
Originated by Chroma Graphics (Overseas) Pte. Ltd.
Printed in China by South China Printing Company Ltd.

13 12 11 10 09
10 9 8 7 6 5 4 3 2 1

New edition ISBNs: 978 1 4329 2531 4 (hardcover)
                    978 1 4329 2548 2 (paperback)

The Library of Congress has cataloged the first edition as follows:
Royston, Angela.
  Life cycle of an oak tree/ by Angela Royston.
    p. cm.
Includes bibliographical references (p.) and index.
Summary: Introduces the life cycle of an oak tree, form the sprouting of an acorn through its more than 100 years of growth.
ISBN 1-57572-211-9 (lib. Bdg.)
1.   Oak—Life cycles—Juvenile literature.
[1. Oak. 2. Tree]
I. Title.
  QK495.F14R68 2000
  583'.46—dc21
              99-046855

Acknowledgments
The author and publishers are grateful to the following for permission to reproduce copyright material:
Alamy pp. **8**, **28 top right** (©David Page), **15** (©David Norton), **22** (©Simon Collings); ©Dwight Kuhn pp. **12**, **28 bottom**; Getty Images pp. **9** (©Ian Sanderson), **20**, **29 top right** (©Michael Melford), **23** (©David Magee), **26** (©Ian O'Leary); Nature Picture Library pp. **11** (©Philippe Clement), **21** (©William Osborn); Photolibrary pp. **4** (©Oxford Scientific Films/Tim Shepherd), **13** (©Oxford Scientific Films/Deni Brown); Photoshot pp. **6**, **7**, **28 top left** (©NHPA/DanielHeuclin), **16** (©Bruce Coleman/Norbert Schwirtz), **17** (©NHPA/Stephen Dalton); Shutterstock pp. **5** (©Shane White), **10** (©Marilyn Barbone), **14**, **29 top left** (©Hydromet), **18** (©Trutta55), **19** (©Paul-Andre Belle-Isle), **24**, **29 bottom** (©Barbro Wickstrom), **27** (©Jens Stolt); Visuals Unlimited p. **25** (©Gap Photo/J S Sira).

Cover photograph of an oak tree reproduced with permission of Shutterstock (©witchcraft).

Every effort has been made to contact copyright holders of any material reproduced in this book. Any omissions will be rectified in subsequent printings if notice is given to the publisher.

We would like to thank Michael Bright for his invaluable help in the preparation of this book.

Contents

ome words are shown in bold, **like this**. You can
d out what they mean by looking in the glossary.

The Mighty Oak

Trees come in many different shapes and sizes.

There are thousands of different kinds of trees. You can tell them apart by the shape and color of their leaves.

Acorn

Sapling

Oak trees grow nuts called acorns.

Every oak tree grows from a **seed** inside an acorn. This book tells the story of how a mighty oak tree grew from a single acorn.

New acorns

70 years old

Hundreds of years old

An Acorn

The acorn has been lying in the ground in the forest all winter. In spring, the Sun warms up the soil and the acorn begins to grow.

A **root** pushes out of the acorn. It grows downward into the soil.

Acorn

Sapling

Catkins

A shoot pushes up into the air. The roots take in water from the soil. The leaves on the shoot open up.

The shoot pushes up toward the sunlight.

New acorns

70 years old

Hundreds of years old

1 Year Old

The young tree is called a **sapling**. The leaves use sunlight, air, and water to make food for the tree.

Water comes up from the sapling's **roots**.

Acorn

Sapling

Catkins

The food keeps the sapling alive and helps it grow bigger and stronger. It starts to grow more twigs and small **branches.**

The twigs and branches grow out sideways from the sapling.

New acorns

70 years old

Hundreds of years old

20 Years Old

By the time it is 20 years old, the oak tree could be taller than a house!

Every year the tree produces new leaves and twigs and grows taller. The twigs become **branches** and the **trunk** grows thicker.

Acorn

Sapling

Catkins

Each bud has new leaves inside it.

Now spring is coming again, and the new **buds** are beginning to open. The buds will open out into new leaves.

New acorns

70 years old

Hundreds of years old

1 Month Later

In spring, the oak tree grows flowers, called **catkins**.

The tree is covered in catkins. The long catkins are male. They are covered in a dust called **pollen**. The wind blows the pollen onto other oak trees.

Acorn

Sapling

Catkins

The shorter catkins are female flowers. Some of the pollen from the male catkins blows onto the eggs in the female flowers. They join together to make new **seeds**.

The wind blows the pollen from flower to flower.

4 Months Later

The new acorns are bright green.

New acorns swell and grow. The **seeds** are inside the acorns. In the fall, birds, squirrels, and other animals love to eat ripe acorns.

Acorn

Sapling

Catkins

Squirrels like to bury acorns to eat later. Sometimes they forget where they have put them! Some buried acorns may grow into new **saplings** next spring.

Squirrels have sharp teeth to help them crack through the acorns' shells.

New acorns

70 years old

Hundreds of years old

6 Months Later

The growth on this leaf looks like an apple.

A **gall wasp** has laid its eggs under this leaf. The oak tree makes a special growth around each egg.

Acorn

Sapling

Catkins

The "oak apple" protects the leaf from being eaten by the grub.

The egg hatches into a **grub**. The grub eats the "oak apple" instead of the leaves. Now the grub has changed into a new gall wasp.

New acorns

70 years old

Hundreds of years old

Fall

Some oak trees keep their dead leaves on their **branches** all through winter.

In the fall the leaves change color. They turn from green to red, yellow, and brown. The leaves slowly dry up and die. Most fall from the tree.

Acorn

Sapling

Catkins

Trees need to rest in the winter to get ready for spring.

The trees in the forest rest through the cold winter. New **buds** form on the oak tree, ready to grow into leaves and twigs next spring.

New acorns

70 years old

Hundreds of years old

70 Years Old

The top part of an oak tree is called its crown.

The tree has now lived as long as some people. Its **trunk** is tall and strong. Many kinds of animals live in the tree.

Acorn

Sapling

Catkins

Oak trees make safe places for baby birds to grow.

Birds have built nests in the tree with leaves and twigs. Thousands of insects live in the **bark** and on the leaves.

New acorns

70 years old

Hundreds of years old

Hundreds of Years Old

Strong winds can knock down big trees.

A storm is coming. A mighty wind whips through the trees. **Branches** crack, and some of the trees are blown over.

Acorn

Sapling

Catkins

Some parts of th
tree have beer
broken off by s

The top (crown) of one tree breaks off and crashes to the ground. The rest of the tree is still alive. It will carry on growing.

Bark is the tree's skin. It protects the wood underneath it.

The tree never stops growing. New wood grows underneath the **bark**. Every year the **trunk** gets a little wider.

Acorn

Sapling

Catkins

This big hole in the tree's trunk will be a good shelter for animals.

This tree is hundreds of years old. The wood in the middle of the wide trunk has rotted away. The trunk is **hollow**—but the tree is still alive!

New acorns

70 years old

Hundreds of years old

An Ancient Forest

The **trunks** of some trees are cut down for people to use.

Very old oak trees can be part of an ancient forest. Some trees die of diseases, but most of them are cut down.

Acorn

Sapling

Catkins

The tree's **branches** are cut up into logs.

Some trees are used to make furniture and houses. Some trees are cut down to make way for roads and towns.

New acorns

70 years old

Hundreds of years old

Life Cycle

Acorn growing

Sapling

Catkins

New acorns

70 years old

Hundreds of years old

Fact File

- There are 450 different kinds of oak tree. Most oak trees live for up to 400 years, but the English oak tree in this book could live for 900 years.

- The **bark** of the cork oak is used to make corks for bottles and cork tiles. It was once used inside life jackets to make them float.

- Oak trees may have 400 different kinds of insects, spiders, worms, mice, birds, and other animals living on them.

- Some oak galls are used to make dyes that are used in making leather.

Glossary

bark hard layer that covers the wood on the trunk and branches of a tree

branches the small twigs grow longer and thicker and become branches

buds small swellings which will grow into new leaves or flowers

catkins long flowers that are covered in pollen

gall wasp insect that lays eggs on oak trees. Another name for gall wasps is gall flies

grub small, wormlike animal that hatches from an insect's egg

hollow empty

pollen fine grains of powder on the male part of plants and trees

root part of a plant or tree that takes in water and food from the ground

sapling tiny young tree

seed male pollen joins with a female egg to become a seed that can grow into a new plant

trunk the main, strong stem of a tree

More Books to Read

Godwin, Sam. *First Look: Science: From Little Acorns... A First Look at the Life Cycle of a Tree.* Bloomington, MN: Picture Window Books, 2004.

Hibbert, Clare. *Perspectives: The Life of a Tree.* Chicago: Raintree, 2004.

Huseby, Victoria. *Oak Tree (Looking at Life Cycles).* Mankato, MN: Smart Apple Media, 2008.

Index